Copyright © 2020 by Pamela Otten

All rights reserved. This book or any portion thereof may not be reproduced or used in any manner whatsoever without the express written permission of the author except for the use of brief quotations in a book review.

Printed in the United States of America

First Printing, 2020

ISBN: 9781653948017

To Kathy with sincere thanks

Proven Tools to Master Your Job Hunt in the Digital Age

BY PAM OTTEN

Table of Contents

Introduction	3
Thank You	6
Tool #1: Gulf Shore Fishing	8
Tool #2: Networking with Your Smart Phone	18
More on LinkedIn	26
Tool #3: HUNTR	29
Tool #4: Out-Maneuver the ATS - Getting to the Interview	44
Using a T-Chart	52
Tip #5: LinkedIn Messaging and Contacts	65
Tip #6: Job History	75
Tip #7: Your Best Self	82
Tip #8: Self-Care	86
Check List to Consider	96
Concluding Thoughts	98

Introduction

This book will give you modern tools and tips for the job hunt that I used throughout my nine-month job search. These tools will apply to you if you are looking for work in these modern times. The "genius" tips are not mine; they were given to me by "genius" experts in various fields as I was learning to navigate the job searching process. I loved learning these tips and so I took them from my notes and put them in this document for you.

I presented these tools at my local job club (Launch Pad Job Club (LPJC), Austin, Texas) in January 2019. You can find a video recording of that talk on my LinkedIn profile page or on the LPJC YouTube channel. The success of that talk generated requests for me to give it several more times in the Austin area – I am surprised how many times I have been asked to give this talk. Post-talk surveys showed the reason for the success is that the approaches I share are novel, relevant, easily applied, useful, and coming from a place of sincere empathy for the time and the emotions of the job seeker. Several job seekers encouraged me to write this short book so I could reach and help more people. I hope my slides translate well into this format and I hope that by reading and applying what you learn in this book you find it easier to get to your next position. I wish you all the best.

I recommend connecting with other job seekers especially if you are unemployed. It helps to commiserate with others during this time. Austin, Texas has three active job seeking clubs – (Launch Pad Job Club is the longest running and the best!) that are free to join and the information presented and connections you make are unsurpassed. People that find a job searching organization regret ever hiring a job coach. Why hire one person when you can go to club, get all the information and resources you need from people with various expertise, and not pay anything? My job club offers classes on resumes, LinkedIn profiles, mock interviews, and more. Additionally, if you are outside the Austin area, look for a job seekers club wherever you live. You will find the support and connection you need to make it through the difficult job searching time. Sometimes local churches sponsor job seeking groups. Wherever you go, you will find this support invaluable. If you do not have access to a club, do access our local Launch Pad Job Club website and YouTube channel where you can watch our weekly speakers encourage, support, and inform job seekers.

Thank You

This book is a thank you letter to my mentor and master job-seeking coach in the Austin area. Her name is Kathy Lansford-Powell and she is the genius behind Launch Pad Job Club. Over the past twenty years she has helped thousands and thousands of job seekers get work. She never charges for her services. Kathy offers the best, most relevant advice and truly is a genius in the field. She will never be thanked enough for the invaluable support she has freely given our community. I am not alone in thinking she is a hero among us. Thank you Kathy, for your dedication to the job-seeker. I hope I have adopted the loving and practical tone in this book that Kathy uses as she works with job seekers.

My job seeking support-friend, Elaine Lange, myself, and my mentor: Kathy Lansford-Powell.

Tool #1: Gulf Shore Fishing

A metaphor is my first tool. It is a true story, like all good fish stories, and it was very helpful to focus on this story as I was job hunting – not only because the hunting metaphor really does apply to the job search, but also because like many good metaphors it can be inspirational to hold on to a vision as you hunt. Even though people who believe in the current "manifestation technology" of our life-work, which essentially means to clarify and envision exactly what/where/when/why/how you want to be in the future to achieve happiness, if you are like me, I just knew – "I'm looking for work" I did not have the "emotional mojo" energy to "manifest" in the ways those books and motivational speakers talk about. Further, the manifestation technology always has us focusing on the "end result": that's exactly how manifestation works. That focus is perfect for your morning mediation, your night time reflection, and those quiet times -- but how do you think about or even get through the day to day? Moment to moment? What do you think about during an interview that is quickly going south? When you hear crickets after applying to 100+ jobs? When you find a typo in your resume? When your allergies act up before that critical phone interview? When you have your dream job in your sights, but then it evaporates and you have to go looking for another? I found ruminating on a decent, motivational-type metaphor helped during the inevitable doldrums. Perhaps you have a metaphor already – here is mine. I hope it helps.

Shortly after being officially unemployed, my dear friend Caryn invited me to her beach-house in Gulf Shores, Alabama. If you have to choose a friend, choose one with a beach house in Gulf Shores. If you have the money, purchase property there. If you can, vacation there. The beach is white-sand, not too crowded, and has spectacular sunrises and sunsets all year round. Each evening we walked down to the beach with our beach chairs and an adult beverage to watch the sun slip away.

Imagine a beach of tourists at sunset. One night a family of about fifteen people from three generations, all in white shirts, cuffed blue jeans, and smiles was having their picture taken by a professional photographer. Meanwhile, standing in the Gulf, there were about five fishermen and some smaller kids fishing from a sandbar not too far out in the water. Up and down the beach, couples strolled, children played, teenagers threw Frisbees. A carefree, perfect ending to a perfect day at the beach.

Then, the sun really began to sink. So, the now-pictured family goes in for dinner and the fishermen and their kids wade in to the shore. Wagons full of fishing gear, day-camping gear, beach toys, and even the life guards pack it in for the night. The tide, which was out, begins to slowly increase in intensity as it begins to roll in. The once flat surface of receding water begins to change direction, ripple with small waves, then bigger waves, then audible waves. The beach empties and the beautiful colors continue to fade from the sky.

At about this time of night - the brief time suspended between dusk and darkness - a tall, tan, ripped, barefooted man approaches some of the retreating fishermen. This man wore sunset-orange colored swim trunks, no shirt -- his shaggy-curly hair blowing off his shoulders. He carried a remarkable fishing pole which looked like an extension of his left-hand. I whispered to Caryn, "primordial man." She giggled.

One of the retreating fishermen pointed to a lone 5-gallon bucket I had not noticed that had been propped up in the sand not far from Caryn and me. I watched as this new fisherman reached into the bucket and with what tool I many never know, fileted a live fish into the size of a salmon steak, threaded it onto the biggest hook I have ever seen, and marched out to the sand bar, heedless of the increasing wave size, the darkening sky, and the sea gulls feasting on the remnants of his gutted fish. Caryn and I gave up our conversation just to watch.

I am not a fisherman but I know some about fishing. I even went deep sea fishing once on a boat, with a bunch of other novice (and similarly drunk) fisher-people. I have done my share of lake fishing. I know how to bait a hook. I have dear memories of my brother fishing and whisper-singing to himself, "here, fishy – fishy – fishy", and how he taught my young sons to fish. In that moment, all of those novice experiences came to bear on how I understood what unfolded next. The fisherman who was now standing in thigh-high, waving water, took his strong arm, well maintained rod, and generously baited hook, and cast perfectly far out into the waves. I counted three heartbeats and on the fourth, the line and rod which were standing straight up, violently surged perpendicular to the water and braced under the fisherman's right armpit. The tip of the fishing rod pointed directly to the sea. The dance/play/fight (whatever you want to call it) between the fisherman and whatever was on his hook began. That whatever was big. I could tell even from that distance. The fisherman worked his end: send out line, reel slowly back in. He kept bringing the fish closer and closer. His muscles were straining. It was exhausting to watch. The fish was huge and would not tire easily. Patience was required. The fisherman's armpit must have ached - in a moment of slack he transferred the rod and braced it in his hip socket. I leaned to Caryn and told her – "that's going to hurt tomorrow." She agreed.

How many minutes could this go on? Big fish have a ton of energy. Five minutes pass. Ten minutes pass. The waves got larger and stronger and were now over the fisherman's waist and hitting his shoulder in increasing size and force. The rod firmly braced and bruising his hip. At about fifteen minutes the fisherman managed to bring the fish in closer. At about twenty minutes we saw his intent was to bring the fish over the sandbar and into the smaller pool directly in front of Caryn and me. We stood, moved our chairs back, and put our toes in the surf to get a closer look.

Our fisherman did it! The fish swam over the sandbar and headed directly for us. Two seconds later we saw the fish clearly: it was not a fish but a shark. We could tell when his dorsal fin broke the water. The shark, which in my estimation was about five feet long, must have sensed his closeness to the shore because he turned 180 degrees so quickly that his dorsal fin snapped the heavy line and he disappeared into the rolling surf. Caryn had stepped back and was standing several feet behind me with her hands over her mouth. My heart was in my throat. It was a remarkable moment. Beautiful really. I looked up. Coming straight toward me out of the waves was one heated and exhausted man in orange swim trunks. I averted my eyes out of respect. "Shark!" he exclaimed. I had to take a breath. That was truly breathtaking. To recover from the scene Caryn and I quietly resumed our seats.

After about five minutes, I finally thought to turn and say something to him. Much to my surprise, he was perched in the sand, systematically repairing his tackle, with the obvious intention to fish again. I said, "that was something" he looked up to me with blue/green sea eyes and spat: "Lady, if you want to see something, stick around, I'm 'bout to hook me 'nother . . . and this time I'm gonna bring him all the way in!" Shortly afterward he marched out into the dark and wave-filled sea.

Oh, the tenacity of the man! Oh, his hope and his effort! Oh, the tools and the tackle! Oh the loneliness! Oh, the mystery of the gulf! Oh, the pending darkness against which the fisherman employs his systematic effort in the unpredictable and (now) broiling sea! Oh! How close he came to the big catch and how far as well! His skills, his tools, his bruises, his streamlined efforts – all (seemingly) fruitless that moment, and much to my surprise, without any rest, there he went, out to the shark-infested waters - back out to fish again!

As a job seeker, don't you feel like my fisherman? Wouldn't you rather have been those folks, smiling for the camera – surrounded by family? Wouldn't you rather be the kind of recreational fisherman fortunate enough to take your kids home for a nice supper? Wouldn't you rather be Caryn and I sipping cocktails and telling stories? Alas, you are not! Why do you feel like the primordial fisherman, intent on fishing in the dark and in the moving sea?

For your job search, can you measure yourself against my fisherman? What kind of tenacity do you have? Are you dressed for it? Do you have the right tools? Do you have the stomach to repair your tackle, bait your hook, and go out again? Do you have a choice? Now, that's the crux of the matter. That is where the books on manifestation leave off. What, if anything, can you choose in this situation? For many of us, you must fish. You must bait your hook and try again and again and again to look for work. You might find yourself bruised and exhausted. You might find yourself working in the dark and the increasing waves when everyone else has gone home. You might have to repair your tackle and try again. Hopefully, one day you can come back to the beach for some casual fishing, a picture or two with your family, a drink with your friend. One day you can just stare out into the Gulf, instead of entering in it.

Until then, picture yourself. You are the fisherman. You step into the unknown. The water has sharks in it. The sharks do not want to be caught. What do you do?

It seems obvious, but if you want to catch a fish, you have to fish. Do not be discouraged. In reality, you can find this primal drive to hunt for your next position, your next "manifestation," your next catch . . . whatever that catch means to you. And, in all probability, your next position will come at a time and in a way that you least expect. Inevitably you might have a story or more about how the big one got away. Hopefully, you will have a great fish story to tell when you hook your next position.

I hope this book gives you some tools, and reminds you of some tools you already have to make your job hunt more of an adventure, than just a process to endure. If you found this book, you are probably already enduring the process, and I do not make light of that since I know its collection of painful difficulties. But, with this strong image, maybe you can choose to enter into the problem of looking for work more like an adventure. A hunt. An endeavor that builds strength.

Maybe when the job hunt is over, you will reach your new position – as I did – with both a relief and a longing. A strange longing. Longing like a person who does "not really" want to go back to job hunting, but does miss the adventure (and to be honest, the battering and recovery afterward) of a good hunt. I wish that for you – and I wish that when you look back on this time of fishing/hunting, you remember that people who watched you go through it admire you, and you should admire yourself as well. Meanwhile, I leave you my fisherman's words: "Lady, if you want to see something, stick around, I'm 'bout to hook me 'nother . . . and this time I'm gonna bring him all the way in!"

Tool #2: Networking with Your Smart Phone

I will be the hundredth voice telling you and repeatedly telling you that networking is the only way to employment. If you really want to work, then start tapping your network. Former colleagues, family, friends, neighbors, etc. There are many videos and books out there that give you tips on how to network and how to attend networking events with confidence. I have read many of these books. I believe in the theory. I think many people read them as well and struggle anyway. The only way to be a networker is to practice. Read the books, watch the videos, but then really – just practice. Go to every event you can stomach and make your small talk. Tell your story. Run your elevator pitch. Tell your story again. Listen to people. Eventually, you will get good at all of it. At some point networking will stop hurting as much, and you will have met great and interesting people – and you will be one of those people.

One master networker and recruiter attended our job club many times to remind us to go to the networking events. Talk to people. His other master advice was to be sure you have a digital copy of your resume on your phone. That way, if you meet a recruiter at an event, you can send your resume immediately. He told vivid stories of people landing jobs that way – on the spot – and with nothing but a few phones between them. People love their gadgets and if you are reading this book, you already know the power of them.

I am from a techy-town so my entire job-seeking community has a smart phone that runs our favorite networking application: LinkedIn. You will need both your cell phone and your LinkedIn application for this particular tool. There are multiple articles (and probably books, too) about how to make your LinkedIn profile, and how to leverage LinkedIn for your job search. I will leave those authors to their expertise. Instead, I will explain a few ways to leverage this powerful app that are less widely used, make you look like a tech genius, and help you break the ice as you network.

Imagine this: You are at a networking event making connections, great! Let us suppose you make a connection and

First, Find Nearby Feature

At the bottom of your LinkedIn screen click on the people icon. This will bring you to your contact management screen.

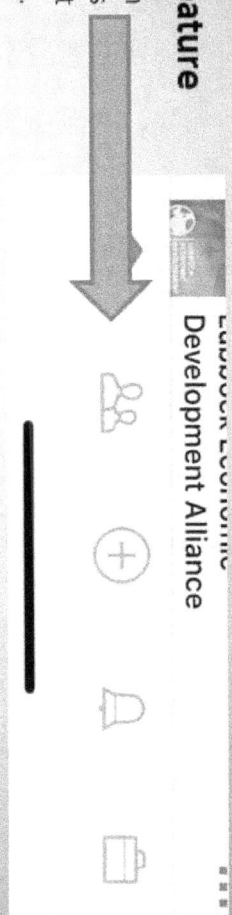

Then, Enable "Find Nearby"

Click on the "Find Nearby" icon to turn it (ON).

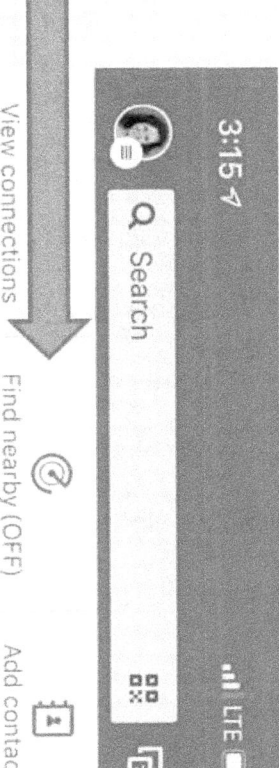

want to connect but would rather not exchange business cards (but do make those as well). You can suggest instead that both of you take the comfort of pulling out your individual phones and opening up your LinkedIn Apps. Then, directly at the top of the screen, in the search bar at the far right you will see a stack of two by two boxes. Click those. You will both need to enable your camera. You will see that a two tabbed, active scanning QR code pops up. One of you needs to keep the scan tab open, the other should click to the QR code. Then, you scan. It does not matter who does which tab, afterward you will see the invitation and once you accept it, you will be connected. I love this method of connecting because of how simple it is and the act itself gets people less focused on each other and more focused on doing this technological thing together. I have rarely met a person who knows how to use LinkedIn in this way. Now that I have taught this to many people, I have noticed that I am remembered because I have taught this skill. It is touching, really – and the point of networking. Give to people! They love it! Be memorable.

Click here to access connection tool

One person click "scan" the other person click "my code"

The second LinkedIn networking tip that you might try in a group setting is the "find nearby" option. First, click the people icon at the bottom of the home screen. Then, under the search box at the top in the middle of the screen is a button called "find nearby." When you enable this feature by clicking on it, your image pops up, and people "nearby" that also have that page open will be able to connect through a friend request by either person. I love this feature if you are networking in a room full of people. If by chance you are running the networking meeting, you may ask people to bring up this feature at the beginning of the event. In that way, people can "see" each other's LinkedIn profiles and decide whether or not to send a friend request. The only trick is that you have to enable your device, and so does everyone in the room to leverage the power of this tool. Technology can bring us together.

Enable Find Nearby

When this screen appears, and other people in the room have also enabled "Find Nearby," their profile connections will appear in a scrollable list in this window.

If you are already connected with someone in the room, a message icon will appear next to their picture/name.

If you would like to connect with new people from this list, a mail icon appears next to each picture/name.

Click to send an invitation.

3:16 √   .ıll LTE

Pam Otten   Nearby   ✕

Nearby members can only discover you when you're on this page

Where is everyone?

Nearby members will appear here when you both have this page open

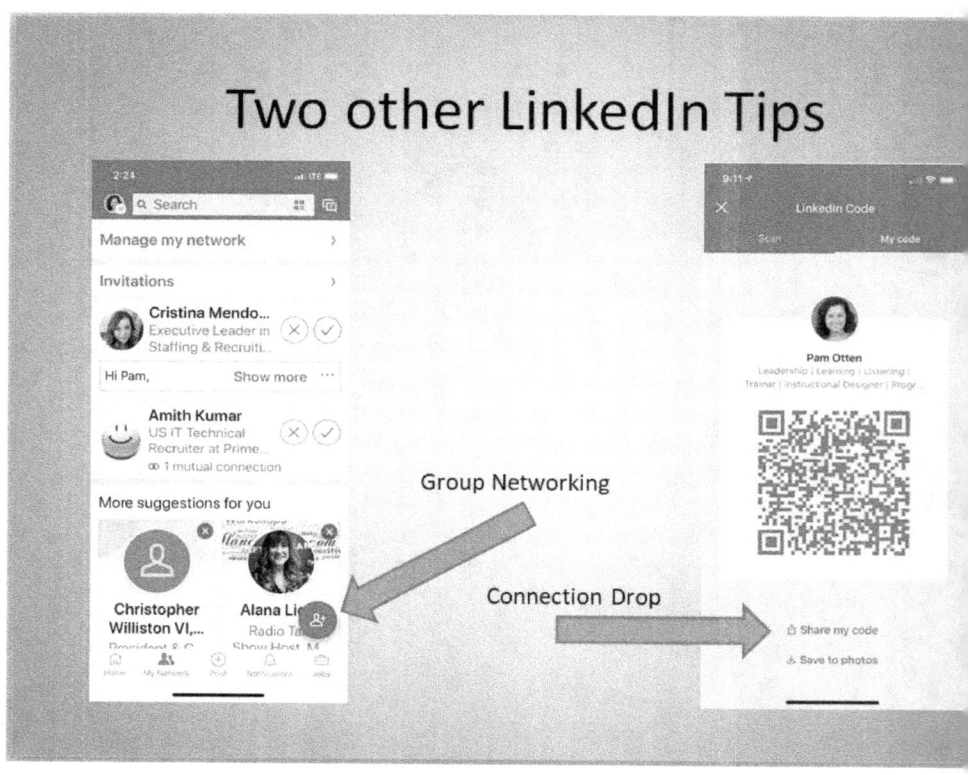

*Now there is a new feature of a "people" button right on the screen. If you click it, it automatically takes you to the "find nearby." You can use this "group networking" button to access your "connection drop" feature as well.

How does this LinkedIn technology fit into the job hunt metaphor? You should leverage all of your tools like the fisherman leverages his rod, line, hook, lures/bait, etc. Keep your tools up-to-date, in good form, and treat them with respect. It is difficult to fish with bare hands. Most modern endeavors are impossible without the right tools. For a job hunt, you do not need many tools, but the ones you do have and the ones you need – well, learn about them and use them! In those moments when you cannot actively "fish" for work – then repair and maintain your tools. Look up tips and tricks on how to maximize your smart phone. Craft your LinkedIn profile.

In my personal quest to maintain my tools, I learned about a GREAT new tool for the job hunt which I will share with you in Tip #3.

More on LinkedIn

I hope by this time in your job search, you have already a strong LinkedIn account and presence. Do manage your LinkedIn profile as you would your resume. Make it strong, updated, and clear. I am not an expert at LinkedIn, so I will leave you to those expert advisors. Seek out the professional tools and videos to bring you up to speed on this important medium. I am by nature very frugal. I chose a few things to invest in during my job search and one was LinkedIn Premium. With the Premium account you can send a certain amount of messages to people outside of your network. Later in this book I will explain how you can quickly find those people you want to send a message to – and what to send in those messages - but here I want to explain what is so helpful about LinkedIn. People who are hiring also tend to subscribe to LinkedIn Premium. Consider this subtle tip. With the premium feature, you can see who has viewed your profile. People, and I am included in this, love to know when other people "look" at their profile pages. So, when you are looking for work, if you want your name to become part of your hiring manager's thought process, be sure to LOOK at THE HIRING MANAGER'S profile. Spend some time viewing the LinkedIn pages of the people who you hope will hire you. The chances they see that you "looked" at them in this digital way are very high. You do not need to enable the Premium feature to do the "looking" but if you do enable it, you may see if those managers "look" at you as well.

ON NETWORKING

Network UP – it is easier to network horizontally. Reach for times when you meet people in position that can help you. Tell people what you need. Take a few chances. Ask for help.

Network now, and learn to do it well – then never stop – we've hit the GIG economy; try to play by those rules.

Do not be the best kept secret in your industry – work on self-promotion.

Be known as the person who is a helpful resource. Be a FRIEND to others and show your face.

Be a "Go Giver" not a "go getter." Read the simple book *Go Giver* by Bob Burg and John David Mann.

You ARE judged by the company you keep; how does your network reflect you? How can you connect with the people you WANT to be affiliated with?

In social media – be proactive, consistent, and cautious. Try to post at least once a week. Also, support your online network with likes and reposts.

Tool #3: HUNTR

Speaking of the right tools ---

Another piece of the job search that can be frustrating (exhausting? Impossible?) is the organizational piece. How do you keep track of all the information that goes into just applying for one job – yet alone many jobs if you do not have a system in place to track your search. If you are a spreadsheet wizard, you can skip this recommendation, but if you are a more visual person, who is inherently "lazy" at organization, then download the free job searching app HUNTR immediately! You will love this app. I looked and looked and trust me - this is the best job searching app available right now. Based on the Japanese method KANBAN, this app will allow you to track your job search with visual clues, smart promptings, and even a robust master calendar to help you keep on track. I feel a little strange even describing this app to you as it is so self-explanatory once you see it. I include a few screen shots in the next few pages to help you see it – but just download it. Again, there are so many user-friendly features in this app, you really do not need me to tutor you on them once you have it; but, here are a few teasers that I LOVE and made me a believer right out of the gate.

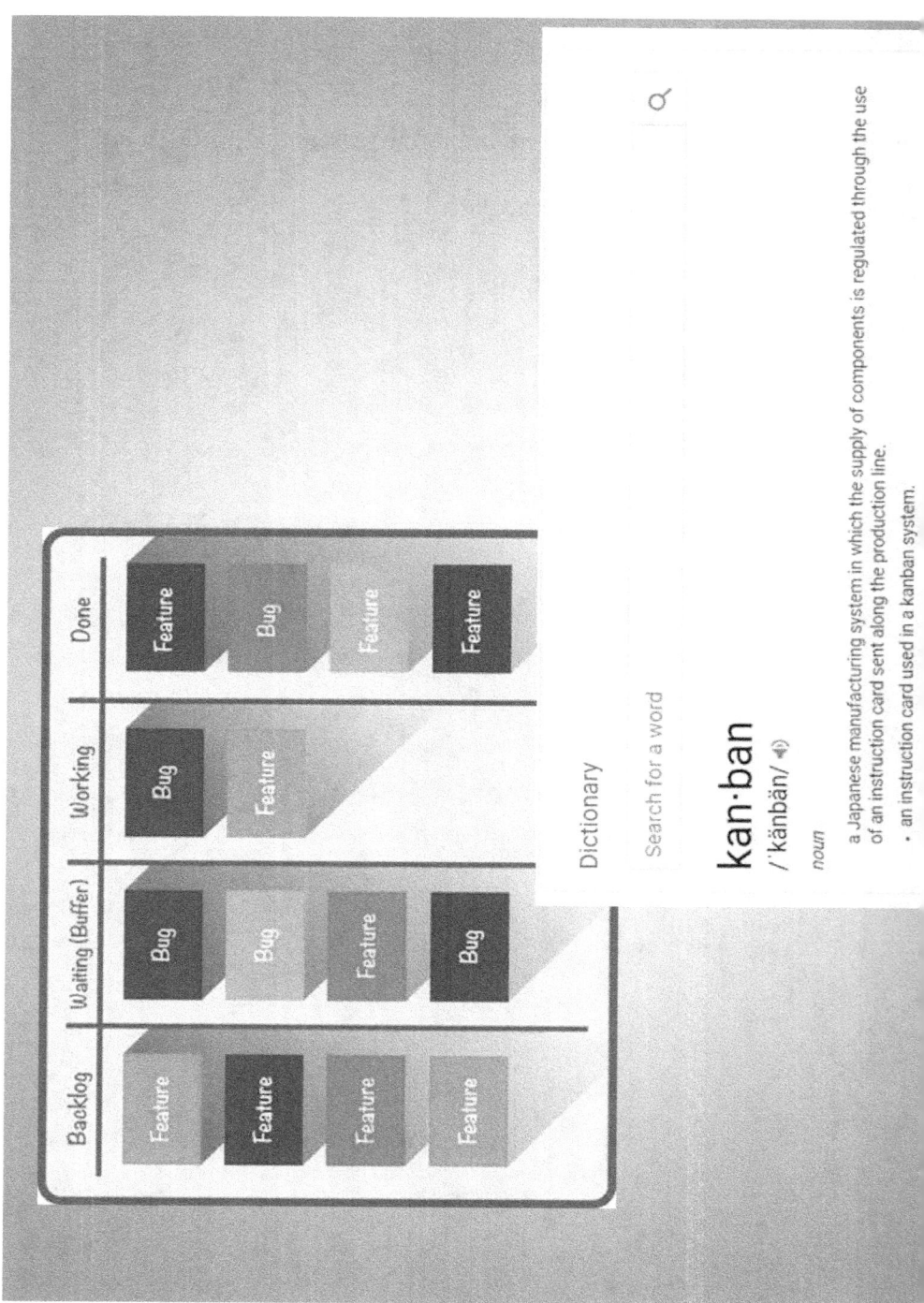

First, you can color-code your job search by customizing the colors of the "job" folders you create. You can find various ways to sort your jobs by color – just as you might use different colors in any folder-organization scheme. One of my target companies was Indeed (based here in Austin, Texas) so I used their iconic blue color. For the state-jobs I went with white. For the other jobs, I used colors from their company logos. Each colored square is movable along the left-to-right trajectory of the job search. Each square is clickable and opens to the files of all the pertinent information and documents associated with the potential job. Gone are your days of trying to remember which resume you sent where. But, that is not all!

For each column – and across each job, Huntr keeps track of all sorts of relevant data for you. You now have personal metrics to gauge your job-search productivity. Further, it prompts you for the information you may not remember to collect otherwise, almost like giving you a personal assistant in your job searching endeavors. If it can fill out the information for you, it does (for most posts it will automatically fill in the company location, logo, and website for you). And, it gives you space to easily copy and paste information and research you collect about the company as you work on your job search.

Huntr your new job search tool: Simple to use, very visual information all in one place

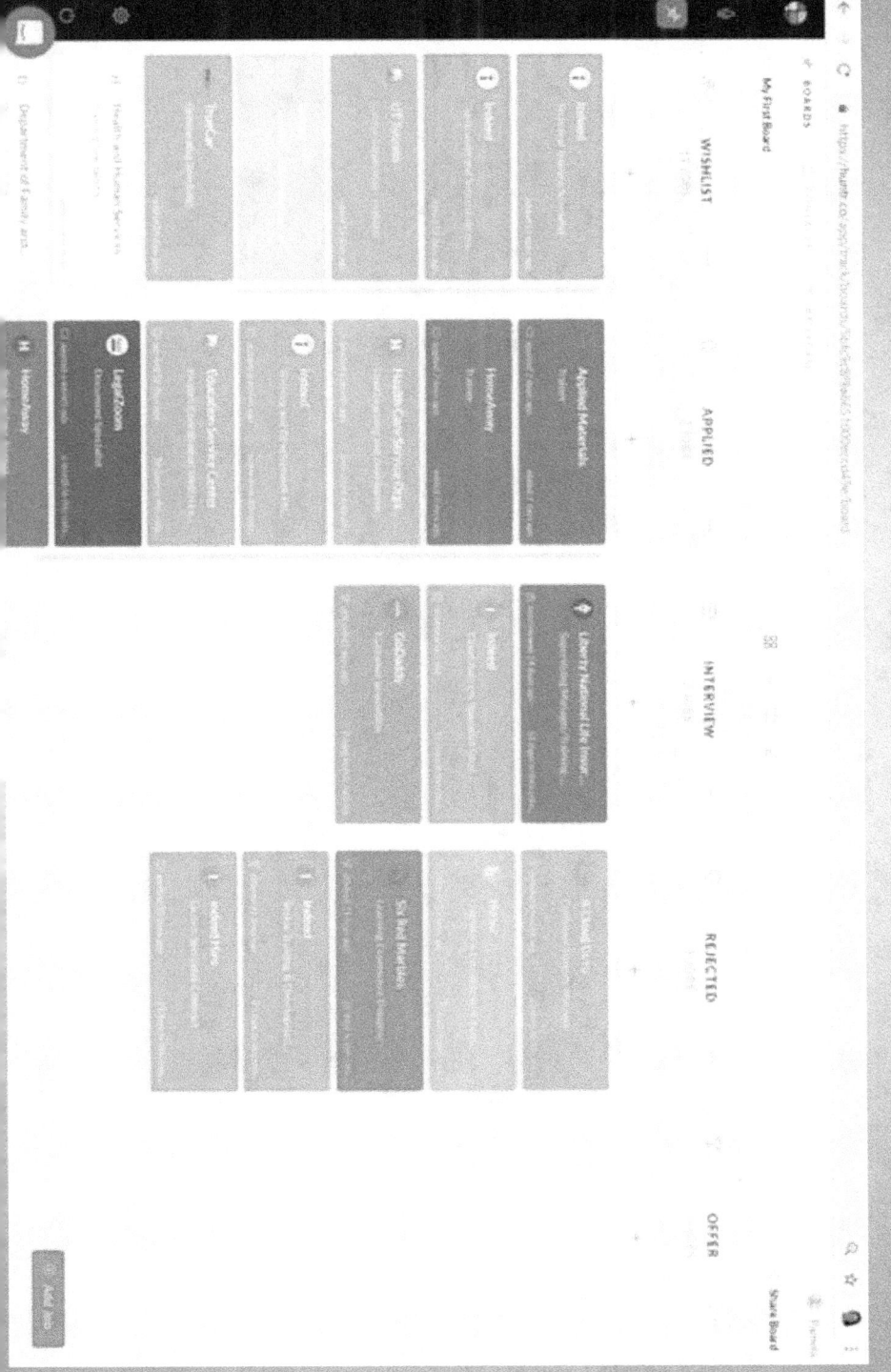

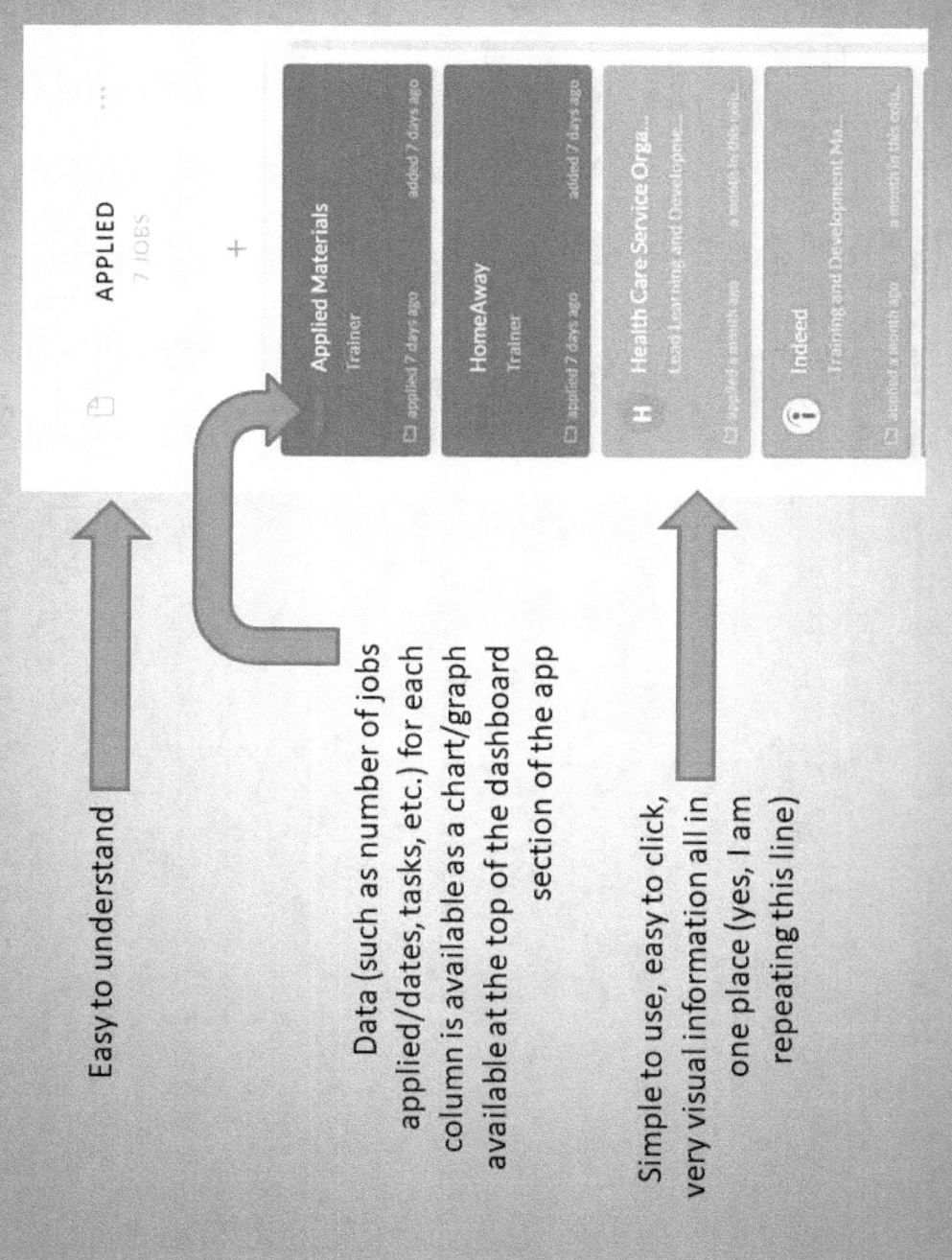

Easy to understand

Data (such as number of jobs applied/dates, tasks, etc.) for each column is available as a chart/graph available at the top of the dashboard section of the app

Simple to use, easy to click, very visual information all in one place (yes, I am repeating this line)

Second, the app has very relevant "suggestions" for each stage of the application process. Use these automatic promptings to let the app build your daily, master job-search calendar and to-do list.

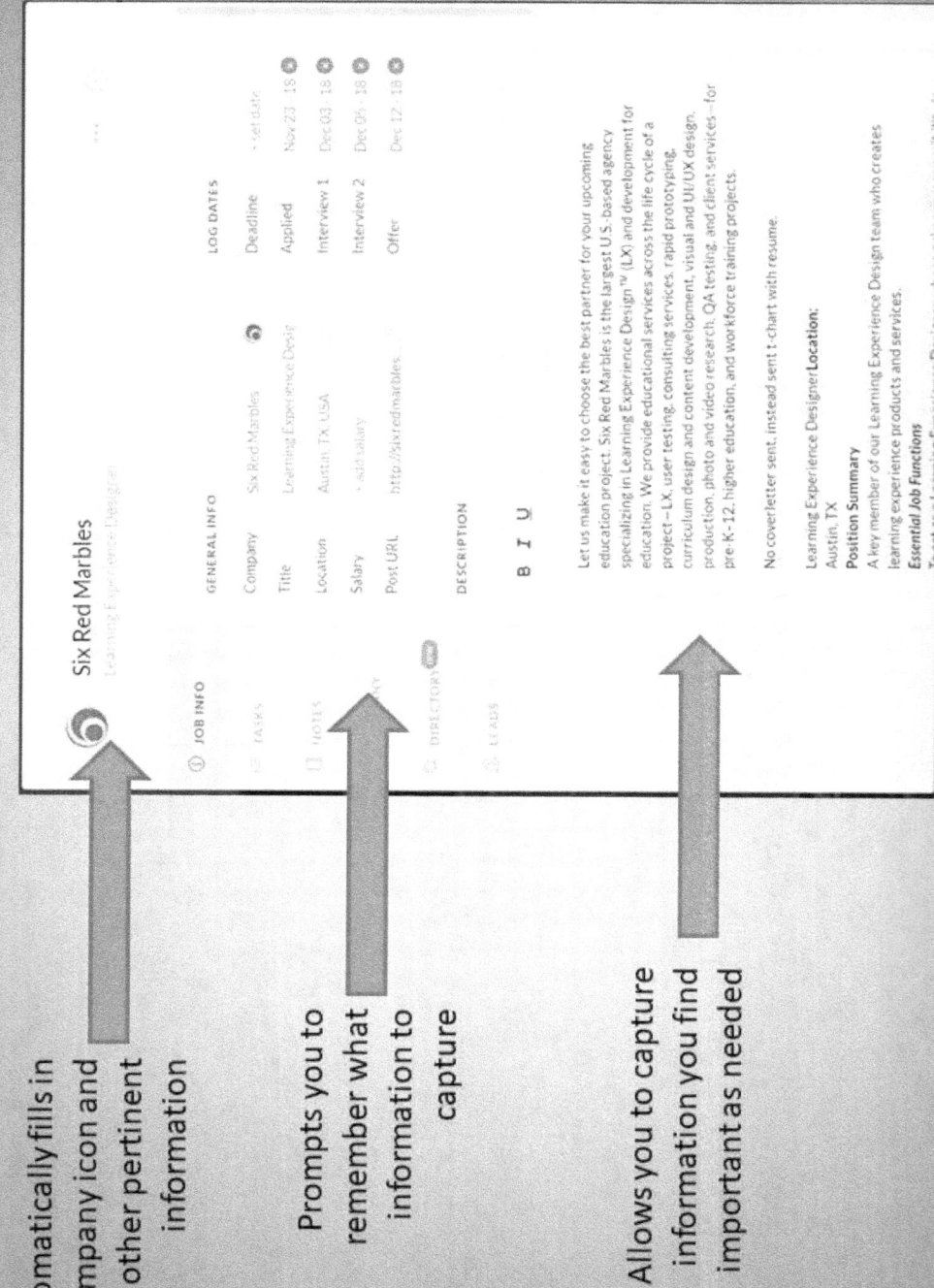

Prompts your thinking about your next steps
(these prompts are from the wish list column)

Navigate through each job folder with sidebar

Make a list of to dos that correspond with a date. This list gets added to a master to do list by date accessible from the dashboard.

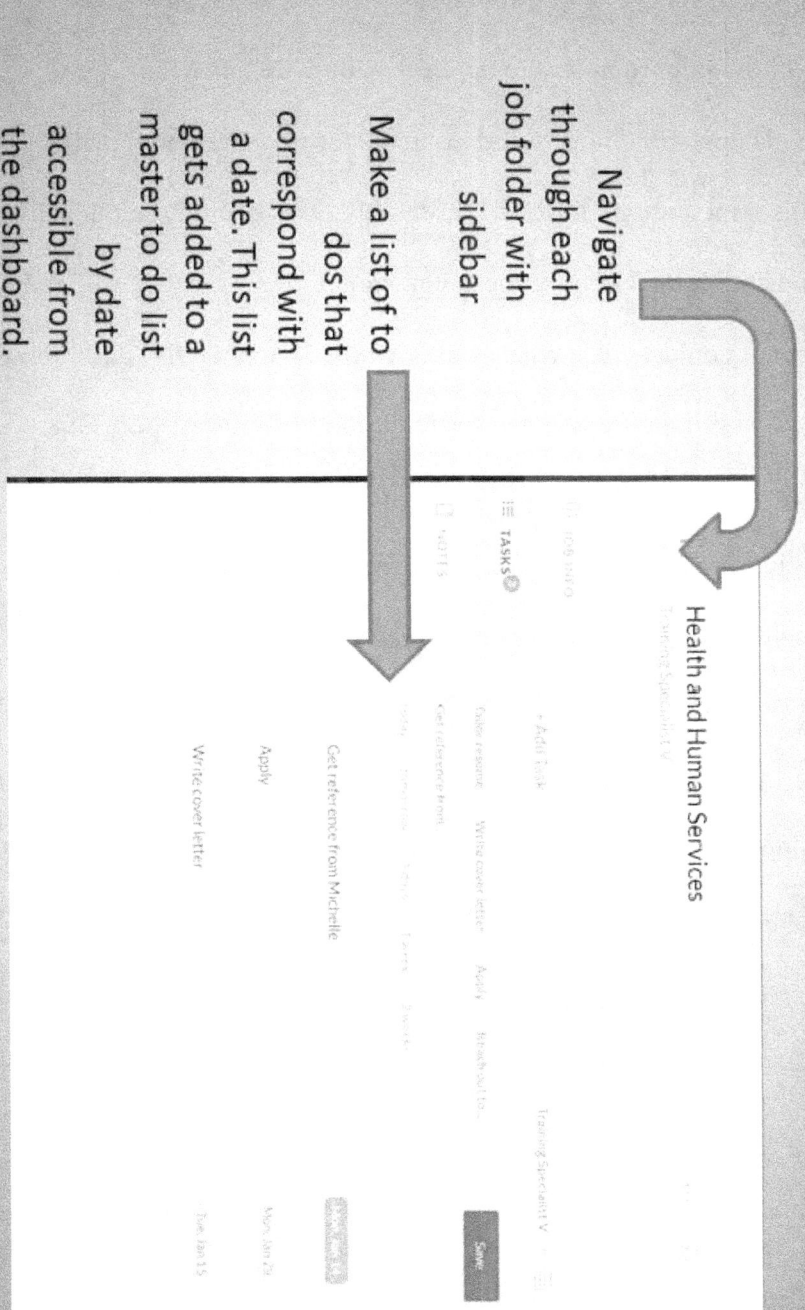

Third, and this is the most astonishing piece about this app that I love, we all know how important it is to connect with people inside the company. This app will "hunt" those contacts for you and populate the contact fields – including a DIRECT EMAIL ADDRESS to the relevant people in the company. Here is where you want to be careful. You get the first three email contacts free when you click the VIEW CONTACT INFO button – the remaining you can pay for in a monthly subscription. But, even without paying for the direct email to the contact, you are given the name and title of the relevant people in the company. Equipped with this information you should be able to reach this contact with a little digging yourself. I used LinkedIn to search for the names of these contacts. Most people use LinkedIn and so they should be relatively easy to find. But, you can simply do your own sleuthing on the company website, the wider Internet, and any other means as you research the people. The contact feature also allows you to do even deeper research on the company, because as you research the people, you can learn so much about the types of people the company hires.

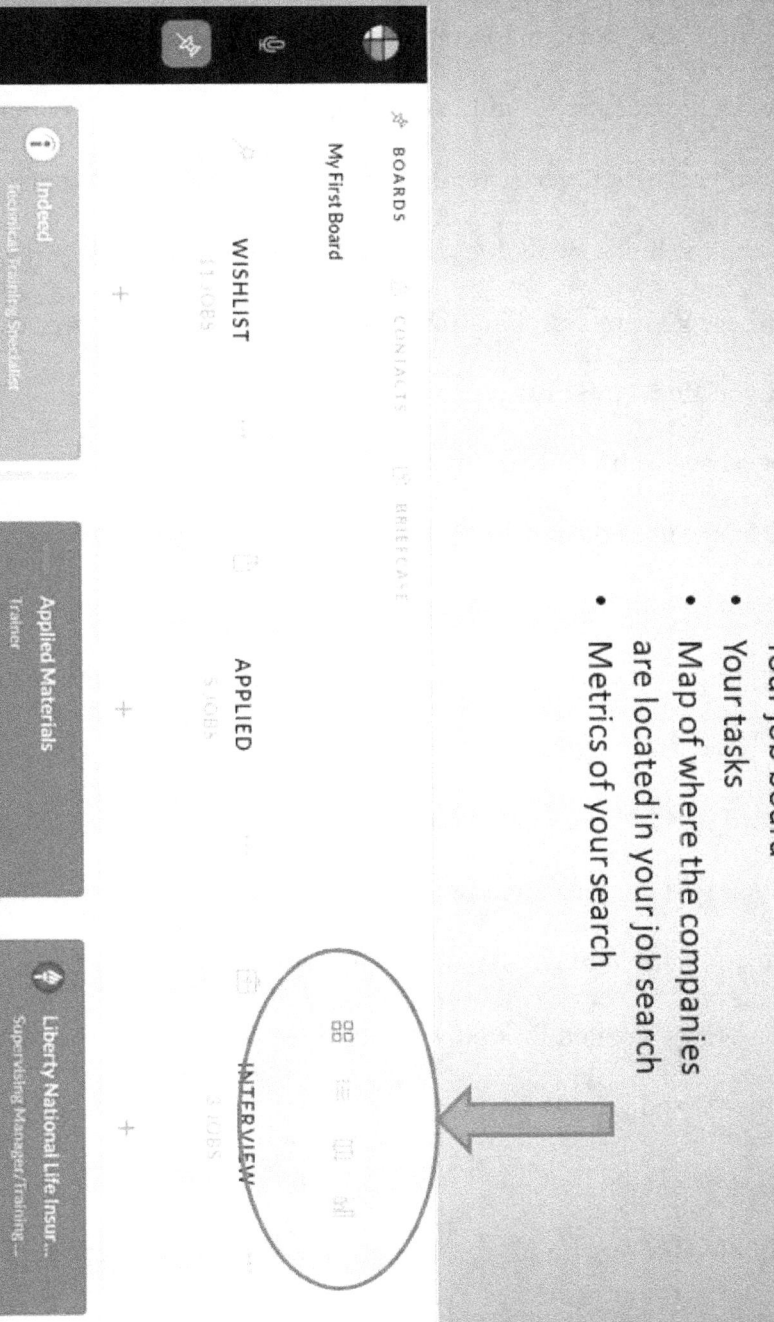

- Your job board
- Your tasks
- Map of where the companies are located in your job search
- Metrics of your search

Fourth, download the app to your desktop, laptop, or phone and install the extension. I was so impressed with this feature. Once you have the extension, you will notice several of the major job searching tools become linked to Huntr. What does that mean? You know that annoying time-sink where you are searching for jobs on an app like Glassdoor or Indeed and you find a job-post you want to pursue – so you save it or flag it or whatever, but then you barely remember what you did with your favorite ones because you're using so many job searching boards, and you are overwhelmed with just reading the job posts? This part of the job hunt is mind boggling. Once you have Huntr's extension installed, as soon as you "like," "save," or flag that post, the job will immediately be copied to your job board in the Huntr app! What a relief! Now you can flag jobs and be assured you will not lose them in the daily grind and the overwhelming nature of the job hunt in the digital age. You leverage Huntr's technology to have a master list created for you with all the information you need to apply for those saved jobs.

In short, Huntr is the best tool I have found to manage my job search. I believe it should take you no longer than any recent app has ever taken you to learn. The entry level price point (free!) is the most useful tool. For a small fee ($7.99/month), you can unlock more contacts and the ability to track more jobs. The free version should be enough for most job searches. I paid for the app because I really believe in it and want to support the author of the app. I reached out to her to thank her for writing it. She is a programmer based in Canada – and seems like a really nice person. I thank her so much for adding this tool to our job hunt tackle box!

Huntr runs seamlessly on your mobile device (not just Apple products)

Screenshots iPhone iPad

Browse the top job sites with one search

Save and track all your jobs in one place

Keep every detail about your jobs

Tool #4: Out-Maneuver the ATS - Getting to the Interview

Standing in shark infested waters –

If you are going to look for work in the modern age, you must remember that you are standing in water with some of the most sophisticated technology on the planet. The ATS stands for Applicant Tracking Systems. If you have not yet discovered this technology in your job search, I am sorry to be the one to tell you (but read on for a solution). In the United States, there are about six or seven different ATS, but they all do the same thing. When you apply for work digitally, your application goes through one of these machines and "scores" your cover letter/resume by matching the posted job description with the words you use in the documents you send to your future employer. Research indicates there are over 200 applicants for each position. No longer does a human being see every submitted document in the first round of screenings for the posted position. Do not imagine that a person reads your resume or cover letter when you press "send." A human person may never even SEE that you sent an application. The human resource professionals with whom I have had the pleasure of speaking or listening speak; have said again and again how they **never see** all the applications. In reality, HR professionals and recruiters **only have access** to the applications that fit a certain percentage of "match words" based on matches between the posted job description and the application. Moreover, this computerized matching is standard operating procedure even if you are applying to a small or medium sized company, especially if those companies are recruiting you through a job board (like Indeed, Glassdoor, Monster, etc.). So, creative resumes, resumes with pictures and quotes, anything unconventional will not get you through to a hiring manager. In other words, if you submit an application digitally, the only way to help your application "stand out" is to use match-words so that your application gets through the ATS.

I highly recommend that you look into a web-based program entitled JobScan. JobScan uses ATS technology to help the job seeker see what the human resource professional sees. It allows the job seeker to get this information and make revisions before submitting an online application. This tool fights fire with fire! A LinkedIn Premium account used to give you access to JobScan, but I believe this is no longer the case. Nevertheless, I highly recommend it! JobScan is an understandable application – maybe it takes a little more effort than Huntr - but again, the effort is worth it. There are great tutorials and an easy interface to get you up and running. In a nutshell, you open JobScan, copy and paste the job posting in the window on the left side, copy and paste your resume in the window on the right, and the computer will do what ATS do – and it will score your application before you send it. Then, you will be able to see how you need to change your resume to meet the job posting. In the pictures that follow, I am not showing you all the features of JobScan – but when you use the program, you will see specific details for each of those findings and how you might correct for a better score. The company is improving JobScan all the time – so please check it out.

JobScan

JOBSCAN INTRODUCTION

Jobscan is a tool that gives job seekers an instant analysis of how well their resume is tailored for a particular job and how it can be even better optimized for an ATS. Just visit Jobscan and either paste in the text of your resume or upload a Word or PDF file, then paste the text of the job posting you're interested in.

CREATE NEW SCAN

Paste the text of your resume in the left box below. Then, paste the text of the job description in the right box. Don't have a resume and job description on hand?

TRY SAMPLE RESUME AND JOB

STEP 1: PASTE RESUME OR **UPLOAD RESUME** | **STEP 2: PASTE JOB DESCRIPTION**

Paste your resume. | Paste the entire job description text - include the Also a Company section

Clear resume | Clear job description

SCAN

☐ Make my resume searchable to recruiters

JobScan is absolutely amazing – it recommends "scoring" your resume to an 80% or over in order to get past the real ATS screeners and land that interview. That is the good news! You have a tool to get past the ATS.

Perhaps, however, you instead have this common scenario: "I have worked so hard on my resume! I am a perfect for this particular job! I know I could land the job if I could just get the interview! I will use JobScan to get past the ATS!" Unfortunately, those of you out there that are using JobScan already have found yourself demoralized even with the use of this amazing tool. You have had the experience that so many people in my workshops have had – you are perfectly qualified for the job and JobScan tells you that your application scores a 30%. Have you been there? OK. Well, JobScan tells you exactly what you need to "fix" to be a match – so you roll up your sleeves and begin to revise your perfect resume. What happens? Three hours go by, four hours go by – yet another scan and you are only at 60%; if you're lucky 65%! How much longer will you invest in this one job application? You are a perfect fit, why can't you get past 65%? Now your once-perfect resume is unrecognizable to you. It is no longer the perfect marketing piece you created; instead, it is a tight squeeze into a job-post straight jacket! Here's a picture of my perfect resume, for my perfect fit job, on my first try with JobScan's help:

JobScan First Try

Jobscan

✏️ Learning Experience Designer

+ SCAN + LINKEDIN SCAN HISTORY RESUME MANAGER JOB MATCHER 🔔 PAM ▾

SHARE ▾   PRINT REPORT

SCAN REPORT
Resume
- Results Overview
- Hard Skills
- Soft Skills
- Other Keywords

Cover Letter
Recommended Jobs

SCAN OPTIONS
- Recognize Plurals
- Star Your Scan
- Exclude Skills

UPDATE RESUME & RESCAN

POWER EDIT DEMO

MATCH RATE

37%

Save Me

Add more missing skills (indicated by ✘) into your resume to increase your match rate to 50% or above.

ATS FINDINGS
✓ 5/5

RECRUITER FINDINGS
✓ 0/0   ⚠ 0/4

SKILLS MATCH
✓ 4/30   ✘ 22/30

FORMAT CHECKS
✓ 1/2   ⚠ 1/2

COVER LETTER CHECKS
0/0   ✘ 0/0

RESUME   COVER LETTER

A few people I have met say that "someone they knew" got past the ATS by taking the required key words and typing them at the bottom of their resume, then putting these words in "white" font to disguise them from the rest of the resume. While tempting, I do not recommend this approach. That ruse has become so common that HR people look for it, and when discovered HR will immediately pitch those resumes. You have integrity and a reputation. Do not take that short-cut chance and blow it.

As a job seeker, I was so frustrated by this experience and the unethical work-around! How can I be a perfect fit for a position but only score 37%? I know that I have the tenacity to work with the technology, but not the wherewithal to forgo all other job seeking activities just to get past the ATS?! Has this happened to you?

Thankfully, one day I had a networking coffee with a semi-retired professional who had paid thousands of dollars to a job coach who told him this amazing maneuver that works to get your application through the ATS – using JobScan but without all the pain. And, it kills two birds with one stone, because it replaces the time consuming cover letter as well. It has worked for me – and works for everyone who tries it. The approach is called a T-Chart (see the example images coming up).

Using a T-Chart

T-Charts have worked for several people who attended my workshops and who I showed how to do this simple workaround. It worked very well for my coffee date, and it works great for that job coach's clients. I know it will work for you. Using a T-Chart you can get the interview and then get the job. Further, in every case the human resource person says how much they APPRECIATE the T-Chart approach because of the clarity of information you provide. And, when you apply for jobs using this T-Chart, you automatically have a document that will help you prepare for and ace your interview.

You will get the interview with the T-Chart approach – but it does ask you to surrender some of your beliefs. First, you do not need a cover letter – you can write one and put it as part of your application, but if there is one place to save time, you can do the T-Chart and replace the cover letter. Second, a computer does not care about length. So, do not worry about length – worry about clarity. Yes, you want to be considerate of your human resources/hiring manager's time, but first you have to get past the computer, and the computer does not care! Once you are past the ATS, the hiring manager wants a good fit, not a certain number of words or pages. The hiring manager needs to makes sure you can do the job – so explain yourself clearly in your T-Chart. Third, stop worrying that an ATS can or cannot read a "chart." Yes, back in the early days the ATS could not read a chart. That is not the case today. The ATS can read charts. The point of making the chart is the ease of reading for the human resources/hiring manager once it gets past the ATS. So, you want your T-Chart to clearly inform and persuade the hiring manager to call you in for the interview. Done right, the T-Chart is the BEST cover letter you can ever write.

To understand the T-Chart you need to understand the ATS. The ATS looks for key words from the job post to appear in the documents of the application. Once there is a close match, then the human resources professional will see the resume. So a T-Chart is simply a document where you have copied and pasted the job post's requirements next to a narrative of how you meet/exceed these requirements. You copy and paste this document on to your perfect resume before or after the resume before submitting it. You would think that this approach would land you 100% score in JobScan, but it will not. But, it will get you above 70% or more easily, and then, your JobScan revisions will take you about five minutes or so because you will only need to change verb tenses or simple words (like managed vs. supervised) in order to score above 80%. It is one thing to describe a T-Chart and another to see the T-Chart. Please see the pictures below for a complete explanation. Using a T-Chart to land the interview is quite like being prepared with the correct pole, weight of line, and bait all at once.

T-Chart Example

Includes the entire list of job requirements on the post

Includes your relevant skills/experience in narrative form

Ends with an enthusiastic request for an interview

Gets through ATS systems because key words match

Works as a great personal preparation document for your interview

At the top you may choose to explain the purpose of the t-chart, but the document itself is self-explanatory. Use the words from the job posting for this line.

My resume follows this document that shows the competencies from your job post matched to my skills and experience.

	Six Red Marbles Learner Experience Designer Job Competencies	Pam Otten skills/experience
1.	Demonstrated ability to col... with...	In my last position, I was... the leadership team that grew a brand-new STEM high school from 180 to 400 students (200% growth) over five years. ... department chair I built and implemented cross-grade level programs while we were small that...
...	...	...
10.	Excellent foundational knowledge of pedagogy and agogy and learning sciences.	Over ten years' experience. While most of my examples above are based off my most recent position with the high school learners I have taught/mentored, I have experience teaching and training adults as well. I have experience developing engaging curriculum outside of the English classroom. Please review my resume and LinkedIn profile for further information. Also, bring me in for an interview – I am right here in SMaG. I would welcome the opportunity to explain further how I can contribute to Six Red Marbles!
	experience.	

Column #1 Number each row

Column #2 Name the company and use the relevant words from their list of requirements

Column #3 Use your name and a relevant heading – use words from their job post

Column #1 This column is important for simple clarity for all your various readers. Your HR person or hiring manager can use the document like a check list. It subtly and purposefully makes you look qualified by sheer volume of the number of job requirements you can speak to coherently. Further, people working with your application in groups can refer to your explanation by number – i.e. "Do you see what she said in #5?"

Most importantly for you, the numbering helps! Many job posts have requirements that are so repetitive that many of your answers to the requirements can cover more than one bullet point. So, instead of repeating yourself in your explanation, simply refer to your prior text by number. You can say then something like: "please see my explanation in row #7 for a clear description of how I demonstrated my ability to bring cohesion to various groups across the corporate structure." Never truncate this response to "please see #7 above" because you do want to continue to repeat key words in this document to pass through the ATS.

Column #2 This column is so important because it actually includes all the key words required to pass the ATS, and it allows the hiring manager to easily scan for particular skill sets. And, it reminds the hiring manager of all the required skills. I loved/hated formatting this column because of the time it took to cut and paste all those key job requirements and get them in a coherent font. But, like baiting the hook correctly, I was precise in the management of making this column as clear as possible. I attempted to leave the grammar errors in this column whenever I could stand it, in order to pass the ATS on that company's terms. Do note that you can have some fun with this column as well. If several requirements are the same, you can put them all in one row. If you would rather reorder the requirements (slightly) to make your narrative clearer, do that. Several times I took language from the job post descriptive paragraph that usually comes before the skill list, and made that part of the numbered requirements to ensure that those key words were hit, and to show I demonstrated that skill-set as well.

Column #3 This column is where you can now show your perfect fit for the job. Include your narrative in your own persuasive writer's voice. Be honest, direct, clear, and informative. If you can, make your points short and to the point. Use the SAR's (situation, action, result) format or any other interviewing-type story telling format to tell how you are a fit for the position. BE SURE to use all the language from column #2 in your explanation. If their word is "managed" do say "managed" not "supervised." Then, you can do all the linguistic things needed to make their requirement fit your story.

    a. You can explain a career pivot, or employ the same language to show how you are a fit:

        "Even though I have not worked as an account professional in the banking industry, I have seven years' experience in the real estate market where I successfully managed ongoing professional accounts and grew my portfolio 250%."

    b. Again, language works when you substitute work experience for a "required" degree:

"While I do not have my bachelor's in computer science, about five years ago, I took several online courses and have been successfully coding in JAVA Script for the past three years. Please see an example of my coding abilities in my explanation in row #3."

c. You can also admit that you do not have exact experience in one of the requirements, but you instead show how you are a quick learner with a desire to grow in that particular skill set:

"My current position has not allowed me to flourish past managing teams of three people, but my desire and recent leadership training has been the spark that has led me to your XXX opportunity."

Again, the more WORDS you use from the job posting in column #3, the easier it will be to pass through the ATS to the interview. Final point: because this document should be your cover letter as well, do use the last sentence to invite yourself in for an interview. Then, when you do get the interview, because you will, you have this document as your springboard to prepare for the phone and/or face to face.

Back to the perfect job. After you build your T-Chart, attach it either as the first or last page(s) of your resume, and then scan it again with JobScan. Be aware, you probably won't be passing yet. Here's my perfect job, using JobScan with T-Chart:

JobScan Second Try after including a T-Chart

Jobscan

≡ Six Red Marbles - Learning Experience Designer

• SCAN • LINKEDIN • SCAN HISTORY • RESUME MANAGER • JOB MATCHER • PAM ▾

SHARE ▾ | PRINT REPORT

SCAN REPORT
- Resume
- Cover Letter
- Recommended Jobs

SCAN OPTIONS
- Recognize Phrases
- Spam Match Scan
- Exclude Skills

[UPDATE RESUME & RESCAN]

POWER EDIT DEMO

MATCH RATE

65%
✓ Good:>86

Add more missing skills (indicated by ✗) into your resume to increase your match rate to 80% or above. ⓘ

ATS FINDINGS ✗ ...
✓ 6/7

RECRUITER FINDINGS ⚠ 1/4
✓ 3/4

SKILLS MATCH ✗ 14/31
✓ 17/31

FORMAT CHECKS ⓘ ⚠ 1/2
✓ 1/2

COVER LETTER CHECKS ⓘ ✗ 0/5
0/5

So, here's where JobScan earns its reputation. Now, I am really close. The only thing I have not done is matched correctly the verb tenses or used the correct words enough to get past the ATS. I have gone from a "red" scan to a "yellow." JobScan is now going to show me all the places where I can "tweak" either my perfect resume or my T-Chart (remember - it does not even know what a T-Chart is it just is looking for word-matches). So, I go back to these documents, make a few changes and this is what happens next:

JobScan Third Try - five minutes later

Jobscan

☆ Six Red Marbles - Learning Experience Designer ✎

+ SCAN   + LINKEDIN   SCAN HISTORY   RESUME MANAGER   JOB MATCHER   🔔   PAM ▼

⟲ SHARE ▾   🖨 PRINT REPORT

SCAN REPORT
Resume
- Resume Finding
- Hard Skills
- Soft Skills
- Other keywords

Cover Letter
- Recommended Jobs

SCAN OPTIONS
- Recognize Plurals
- Start Your Scan
- Exclude Skills

UPDATE RESUME & RESCAN

POWER EDIT DEMO

MATCH RATE
✎ Guide Me

Great job!
You've reached 80% and increased your chances of being seen by a recruiter.

87%

ATS FINDINGS   ✗ 0/2
✓ 7/7

RECRUITER FINDINGS
✓ 1/1   ⚠ 1/3

SKILLS MATCH
✓ 26/31   ✗ 5/31

FORMAT CHECKS
✓ 7/8   ⚠ 1/8

COVER LETTER CHECKS ⓘ
0/0   ✗ 0/0

RESUME   COVER LETTER

With everything you have to do – do not in any uncertain terms try to get to 100% for any job with JobScan. That may take you forever and will not be worth your time. Once you get a "green" score (80% or above) you can be assured that your application will reach a human's hands. Then, you will have a fish on the line. What happens next is part of the alternative reality of the job searching process – the fish may spin around and cut the line – meaning you may have a government shut-down take the job away from you (like this one I am showing you), there may be a switch in the company, the job may close without your knowing it, there may have been an internal applicant all along, another applicant really may be more qualified, the job post may have changed overnight – you do not know, and may never know – but one thing is for sure, you have beaten the ATS. If your bait holds and the waters are in your favor, you will feel this fish on the line by the receipt of a phone call or email! You would be so surprised at the power of the T-Chart.

Tip #5: LinkedIn Messaging and Contacts

Casting out for the perfect job –

Let us now agree that you are ready to apply for a position in a company. This position suits you! You have found an open position, or at least you know the company is actively hiring. You have done your due-diligence and have researched the company. You looked through your personal network to see if anyone you know works there. You have used the contact feature in Huntr to familiarize yourself with various people in the company and the roles and positions. You are ready to build your T-Chart and beat the ATS. So, now, what is next? How do you make initial contact? How do you cast your bait?

Recruiters, human resource professionals, and people in my network have told me over and over again that people, in general, forgo the obvious step of reaching out. Why? I think it is because people assume that the "application" route that the computer puts you through to apply is enough. But, it is not. There are still real people out there attempting to fill real positions. As baffled as you may be by the technology that brings people to their attention, they are similarly overwhelmed by the technology that pushes the "right" candidates to them. Human contact – the person on the end of the fishing pole – will make or break your job search – so you might as well be the first person to reach out. Whether you use LinkedIn or you use Huntr to get a direct email say something to people in the company -- cast the line. Knock on the proverbial door. What do you have to lose?

So, what are you supposed to say? If you know someone who works at the company, of course, reach out to that person first, if it makes sense. An informational phone call or coffee seems to work best. Most people in your contacts will gladly take a fifteen minute phone call especially if it is prearranged in text or email. You want to keep these phone calls and coffees pertinent. Make a list of strong questions. Make a little small talk, ask your questions, and make "the ask" for an introduction to the hiring manager. Do not be afraid to solicit help. You are job seeking, and in today's economy if you are hired based on an internal referral, your contact may make a small bonus, so it never hurts to ask.

If you do not know someone in the company, then use your Huntr contacts to scour LinkedIn for the pertinent people's LinkedIn profile. Again, as I suggested above, be sure to "look" at the profiles of people in the company to make them aware that you exist. As a member you should have the ability to send a few emails directly to a person outside of your network. With LinkedIn Premium, you have about ten free contacts a month. Depending on the rank of person you are trying to connect with, using this direct contact is a strong way. LinkedIn is a professional networking platform, so sending your introduction in a short, professional way will generate some interest in your application.

1. Human resources connections - with human resource personnel – the gate keepers – the best way I have found to use LinkedIn is to simply send a connection request with a note that promotes your application. Something simple – there is a word limit - in about three to four sentences like:

    Good morning Heather! I just submitted my application for your open position on your (xx) team. I really love what your (xx) company does in this space and I know my experience and enthusiasm (use your words) for the position would bring (solve, resolve, etc.) the (indicated something specific here from the job post like: professionalism you request) in your job posting. I look

> forward to connecting with you here. Please let me know if my application is complete. Have a great day!

You will be surprised at the response you get with a friendly connection request like this. Even if the HR person does not accept your request or respond to your note, you will find that they look at your LinkedIn profile. To be honest, when I have sent notes like this, I always get a response from HR.

2. Hiring manager connections – These notes are trickier because you are maintaining your enthusiasm and professionalism, while adding value to the time the hiring manager takes to read your note. Along this vein, I would not send a connection request to a hiring manager. Instead, I would send a direct message either through LinkedIn or direct email using Huntr to find the email address. Here you may try a note like this:

> Good morning Christine. Your company's mission directly aligns with mine, so I was enthusiastic this morning as I submitted my application for the open position on your team through your online portal. It seems that from your

post you hope to find a person who (does x). Recently I (insert a relevant professional win here from your resume such as: saved my current company x dollars by creating xxx) among others. Currently, I am actively seeking a new position and would welcome the opportunity to speak with you at your convenience. Have a great day.

Then, if you can, include a link to your LinkedIn profile, your resume, and your T-Chart. If the person wants to open these documents, they are there! If not, they are digital and do not do any harm to the hiring manager. If you have a very strong, very short elevator pitch, this is where it goes – written out and directed to the hiring manager.

You can never go wrong sending notes to people if the notes you send are ones that are meant for genuine connection. If you are gracious and generous, the people you're connecting with will be gracious and generous back. So, when you do make it in for an interview – be it a panel interview, a one-on-one, a phone interview, a video interview – it is always appropriate and I would say, mandatory, that you follow up with a thank you note. There are books and articles with actual words you can use to generate these notes, so find them out there! But, be sure that within 24 hours of a genuine contact with a person, you follow up with a genuine response. Even if you decide you do not want the job or you are rejected for the position – it does not matter. Follow up and thank the people for their consideration. It is the human thing to do – and it works so well in your favor. The energy and effort it took for you and the other people to come to the table and meet is tremendous. If the hiring manager or HR person likes you, you will be considered as positions open up in the company. I know of several people who landed their dream position because the person who was initially hired did not work out for some reason. I know of people who landed a different position in the same company. I know people who got the position because it was eventually split from one into two positions. You never know what is going on behind the scenes in the company. Be patient and be assured that if you were given the face-to-face interview, you are most likely a match for the company. Take heart, and make your notes genuine.

Start with LinkedIn (or a direct email from Huntr)

Katie Edenfield, CSP
Recruiting Coordinator with Honor In-Home Care

NOV 26

Pam Otten · 3:35 PM
Learning and Development Job Application

Hi Katie - I am personally aligned with the mission of your company - Honor. I submitted my application last week on Wednesday and would welcome the opportunity to discuss. I know the hectic nature of start-ups, so in the event that my application crosses your desk in the next few days - I wanted to you to know my enthusiasm for the Learning and Development Associate position. Have a great week! - Pam Otten (applicant)

NOV 30

Katie Edenfield, CSP · 4:24 PM
Hi Pam,

Thank you for reaching out and sharing your experience and connection to our company. I just sent you an email so we can find a time next week to connect.

I look forward to it.

Pam Otten · 4:44 PM
Me too!
Thank you,
-Pam

Amanda Casarez
Corporate Recruiter at LegalZoom

Pam Otten · 3:22 PM

Hello Amanda - I recently applied for the Document Specialist position in Austin through LegalZoom's website. I believe in the mission of LegalZoom and would love to become part of the Austin-based team. Thanks for your consideration and have a great day! -Pam Otten (applicant)

DEC 16

Amanda Casarez is now a connection

72

Follow up with handwritten notes and email

Thank you & Follow up > Inbox ×

Katie Edenfield <katie.edenfield@jonhonor.com>
to me ▾

Thu, Dec 13, 2018, 12:28 PM

Good Afternoon Pam,

Happy Friday Jr! I hope you have had a great week so far. I wanted to reach out and say thank you for sending the hand written letter. I appreciate your thoughtfulness and kind words.

You have great experience and a personal connection to Honors mission which are 2 key things we look for. I did pass your resume along to my manager so we can keep you in mind for any new roles that may be a fit. Please do check out our Careers page and if there's anything you see that is of interest send it my way.

Best of luck to you and I wish you all the success.

Kindly,
Katie

↩ Reply   ➡ Forward

See, you have to want to GET the fish, but you cannot believe that fishing is a straight line. It is a hunt. You must put yourself out there – but you must not collapse when the fish on the hook gets away. You persist. You cast again. You continue to show up with your best self. Eventually, there will be a fish on the line. Your fish. Your job. Do not lose integrity over the fishing itself. The best way to land the job is to continue to do you in the best way possible. Eventually, you may have more than one fish on the line and you will have decisions to make then! Practice your integrity whether the answer is yes or no.

Tip #6: Job History

I am not an expert resume writer, and again there are great resources out there for putting a strong resume together. Look at those resources for your best advice. If you have the money, you can hire someone to write your resume for you. Do what works best for your situation.

As I applied for posted jobs, I found myself so frustrated by the rigidity of the application process. Beyond just knowing that the ATS was going to scour my resume, inevitably there was also a long drawn out process of entering my work history – in years and months - as another part of the process. This rigid format felt so offensive to me, and may to you. Perhaps you are attempting to transition out of one industry and into another. Some of you may be re-entering the workforce after a long illness, caregiving, or in general – just took some time off. Maybe your job search went long. Today, you will find that many companies have these new application systems that ask you to type in a chronological work history – what do you do if the last time you worked was three years ago? Or, what do you do if you want to re-enter the workforce but with skills from a position you held several jobs or several years prior? Some of you, like me, want to present a mixed resume with your most relevant qualifications at the top and your work history at the bottom – so these new systems frustrate your presentation. Truly, it is a confusing (and rigid) time to be looking for work. What I mean is that so much of what is being collected from you as the job seeker is so rigidly done, that you may feel as though you are not the one in control of the presentation process.

My recommendation is two-fold. If you are just looking for work in the same industry, this advice is not relevant to you. Just know that when you are applying for work, you will probably run into this requirement, so have your resume on hand to copy and paste all the relevant information as you apply. But, if you're like me you may have to get creative with your presentation even in these rigid systems. I say, embrace the gig economy.

So, if you spent your life as a homeschool coordination genius (I recently met a woman who did this) but never earned a dime doing that, how does that go on your resume? AS EMPLOYMENT. Get your dates correct and put those skills and the duties on there. You do not have to simply list the jobs where you earned a W-2. In my case, I had a series of remarkable jobs and internships from a decade prior that I wanted to showcase. Further, I had been unemployed for several months, so I had been doing some freelance work for various people as I was job searching. So, I combined these positions into my own personal consulting company, resurrected them as multiple clients, had the dates available, and moved this information to the top of my resume under a long-standing consulting company titled with my own name. Obviously, I put those experiences as the most recent part of my resume. That solved my relevancy problem, was honest, and allowed my jobs from the past to shine at the top.

To illustrate, here's a picture of my original resume:

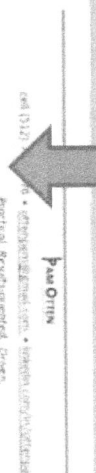

Here's a picture of my revised resume that allowed me to put more relevant work experience on page one.

Resume includes customized objective and "sells" the applicant

Resume updated to include current, temporary role

As for long gaps, employers are becoming more and more tolerant of workers who take time off to care for self and others. If you can show you have learned something, contributed something, or somehow made the world a better place – then do not leave a "time gap" on your resume at all – especially in those rigid application gatherers. Find a way to simply state what you were doing during the gap – give yourself a relevant title, identify the relevant dates, and be honest about what you learned and accomplished. I cannot stress enough that your application is a marketing document, which requires honesty (who wants to work for a company that doesn't value honesty?), clarity, and you putting your best foot forward. Think about how you would like other people to see you as you worked through this employment gap. Then, articulate that on your resume and even when you need to type an accounting of yourself using dates and accomplishments in online applications.

Tip #7: Your Best Self

If you are in the midst of a job search next to the overwhelming organizational piece, the second most frustrating aspect to integrate is the self-awareness piece. Too many of us just need a "job" and the self-help books out there on this topic may keep us from entering into the job search because they require us to do all this self-exploration first. In a perfect world with no bills to pay, this self-exploration sounds absolutely wonderful! I have read those books and do understand their approaches. In fact I do that work, and hope someday to be self-aware enough to be able to fish only for the perfect job instead of taking whatever gets on the line. But, to be perfectly honest, as a person out of work, I would be super excited to land any fish. I may not pack up my tackle and go home entirely; I might hold out for the perfect job -- but, to pay the bills I may really take a hard look at what gets on the line. It may be enough. I may not stop fishing entirely, but I am going to spend the energy making the fish-I-catch work. I may actually settle. I am not proud when it comes to feeding my family. Also, I am old enough to know that the "perfect" job does not exist. Further, I know to get a fish I have to fish – I have to cast. That is a requirement.

All of that being said, there is wisdom going into the job search with self-awareness. There are several wonderful books to help you get started on this path. But, I would argue that if you have been in the work force for any length of time, you have already done this work. What I recommend is that you do not do the self-awareness piece from a blank sheet of paper! Instead of tracking down the latest "uncover your passion" book or manual, why not instead look backward at your history that has already been written? Dust off your old performance reviews. Read those. Find one of those tests you have already taken at a prior workplace – the Clifton Strengths Finder, the MBTI test, the Color Code test, etc. Review those. I have found these prior tests and evaluations do a few things. First, I remember what I have accomplished and what value I added to teams and workplaces. I do not underestimate myself. Then, when I look at the results of those national standardized tests, I am able to see my strengths and weaknesses. These help me prepare for those interviews. I can confidently explain myself with a simple review of these materials. I can answer the weaknesses question with language already provided from these assessments. Alternatively, if you cannot find these documents in your personal files, just register and take one of the tests below. Some versions are free. Then, you do not have to "reinvent" yourself in some prescribed way. Take the test, read the results, then go fishing. You do not have to reinvent (unless you want)! If you are reading this book, you may not be an expert in self-awareness – please do not beat yourself up about this. If you are fishing for work, fish for work.

What are my strengths?

REMIND YOURSELF WHAT YOU ALREADY KNOW ABOUT YOUR STRENGTHS AND WEAKNESSES THEN USE THIS INFORMATION IN INTERVIEWS

You can find most of these tests on line but you may have already done them – check your personal (and personnel) files.

- Myer's-Briggs
- Clifton Strengths Finder
- Standout 2.0
- 16 Personalities
- Color Code
- The Advantage
- Personality Perfect
- Etc.
- *Your prior work evaluations*

Tip #8: Self-Care

Recently I heard our expert job coach, Kathy Lansford-Powell welcome new people to Launch Pad Job Club. At one point she explained that these job seekers are now in an "alternate reality." She said that as a job seeker you can be the best prepared, the most qualified, the best interviewer, the perfect candidate, the most connected, etc. – and still not get the job. Kathy went on to say that as a job seeker things that should make sense do not always make sense. The reasons for not catching a position are as countless as the reasons you do not always catch a fish when you fish. Accepting this alternate reality is the most difficult part about job seeking. Kathy has been coaching job seekers for over twenty years – I could not agree more with this wisdom. Job seeking is the most difficult job I have ever had and the most stressful. Besides the physical, mental, organizational, time-consuming, and technical work it takes – the emotional beating is brutal and relentless. Further, each one of us experiences the beating differently based on our life circumstances. There is no right way to survive the search. Job seeking is truly an alternate reality.

What alternative reality are you living through right now? I had several indications that I was outside of reality when I was a job seeker. One of the most brutal for me was the amount that I could "not" accomplish during the day. In contrast to when I worked, when I could easily accomplish ten to twenty significant items on my to-do list in a day – significant as in job-related, personal, family maintenance, etc.; as a job seeker if I could get to four to do's on my list, that was a big day. I never got to the bottom of that statistic, but I am certain not being able to accomplish as much in a day was part of the alternate reality. I witnessed this skewed reality even further the closer I came to getting a position. At times the reasons for not getting a job I had on the line were so convoluted and strange, that I am still grappling with some of the loose ends. I know I will never completely understand why I was passed over for several positions. Those stories are part of the fishing expeditions that I alternately embrace as part of the great "fish story" and cringe at when I think about the jobs that got away. Sorry to digress.

To balance this stress, you must not roll your eyes and tuck deeper in denying yourself self-care. It is counterintuitive but essential that you have fun, laugh, get decent sleep, nourish yourself, exercise, connect with others, seek medical intervention if you are depressed or ill, and do everything that you need to do to ensure you do not collapse under the stress. At my job club, Kathy prints a weekly list of many free events and low-cost activities to do in town. That list shows how essential her advice is. Whatever it takes, you must balance the stress. Create a new-normal while you are job seeking so that the rest of your life does not fall apart. Can you thrive in the midst of a job search? I would hope that could be the case! You should definitely think about in what areas of your life you can thrive – not just survive – during your job search.

IDEAS FOR PRACTICING
SELF-CARE

PHYSICAL
go for a walk
dance
hike
swim
get a hug
play with a dog
clean & reorganize your room
take a bath

MENTAL
read a book
learn a new skill like photography or drawing
do a DIY project
color
turn your phone off

EMOTIONAL
meditate
practice Yoga
light a candle
talk with a friend
go on a date
journal
write down a list of things you're grateful for

Take care of YOU!

- Health: diet & exercise
- Wardrobe & hairstyle
- House & Home
- To Do Lists
- Rest
- Enjoy your "time off"

Besides the tangible "to dos" that will help your stress levels, the best advice of self-care I can give is to remain as mentally positive as you possibly can. Read about manifestation and how your thoughts manifest your reality and you will agree that your thoughts do influence your reality. Manifestation is easier said than done. Come up with a daily ritual that allows you the freedom to think positive thoughts.

To that end, especially during my job search, I turned off the media (though I love to listen to the news), and I reworked my standard topics of interests to leave room to find some new ways of thinking. I now subscribe to a few uplifting, easy to read apps and blogs that have fresh content pushed to me daily. These keep me motivated. I love the Daily Quote phone app because it gives me one positive thought from a thought-leader to think about each day. I enjoy Seth Godin's blog because he always makes me think even deeper about what motivates me and others. I love the Daily Stoic blog because it reminds me how to genuinely be in the world.

For job-seeking insight I follow Liz Ryan on LinkedIn because she speaks the truth about current hiring practices. She has been a tremendous help to me and thousands of people. She is a frequent writer for Forbes Magazine. To learn about the recruiter's perspective, I love the straight-forward writing of Alan Karpiak. If you look him up, you may have to dig a bit to find his articles, but they are all exceptional and tell many inside stories of how recruiters think and operate. I hope a few of these suggestions may work for you – but even if they do not – I do hope that you take this time to find a few new topics for you to learn that are outside of your traditional interests.

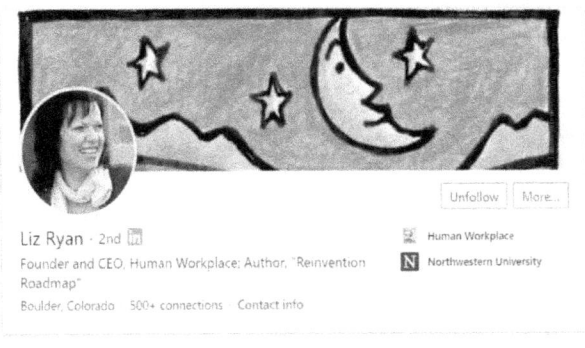

Liz Ryan: https://www.linkedin.com/in/lizryan/

Seth Godin: https://www.sethgodin.com/

Adam Karpiak:
https://www.linkedin.com/in/akarpiak/

Daily Stoic: https://dailystoic.com/

Take care of you by connecting

- Visit with people, nature, yourself
- Visit with Indeed at LPJC
- Get an updated headshot
- Go to the other job clubs
- Go to the networking events
- Go to Product Camp
- Go to any event anyone invites you to
- Help other people find work/stay positive

Take care of you by staying inspired

- Feed yourself positive messages (turn off the negative)
- Surround yourself with healthy people
- Surround yourself with and support other job seekers
- Celebrate the "job getters" because soon you'll be joining them

Check List to Consider

I am a visual person who also needs some external (non-digital) updates on my progress. To that end, I made and copied several of these check lists as a way to keep track of my "hot jobs" and ensure that I understood the progression, depth, and fortitude it takes to fish. Here is my list:

CHECK LIST WHEN APPLYING FOR A JOB

Potential job? Yes!
Register the job on Wish List at Huntr
Get to work:
- Confirm that the job is still posted on the company website
- Research until you find a contact - use LinkedIn or Huntr
- Create a desktop folder for this job
- Copy and paste job description to a Word doc
- Build a t-chart (and/or access JobScan)
- Tweak your resume for the job
- Double check all documents and save them in your folder
- Send your application
- Reach out to your contact—tell them you've applied

Update Huntr lists and make new appropriate "To Do" lists
Research the company – take good notes
Research the salary range – take good notes
Follow up on your application in one week (use Huntr to track this)

Concluding Thoughts

When you are connected with people who are also job searching help them find work as well! Then when/if they land work before you do, be gracious and excited for those individuals. It is essential that we support each other in the journey until the end. Congratulate them. Wish them well! And, for all the work you did to connect with them initially, be sure to stay connected now. Your friendship may lead to your next position – but that is not the point. The real point is that your friendship will always serve as a testimony to the alternate reality you were in when you were looking for work.

When you do land your next position – negotiate your start date to be a Wednesday or a Thursday so you can meet all the new people, get your land legs, and have the weekend to recover before you tackle a five-day work week right away. Obviously, adjust for your circumstances, but if you can – a few days buffer to get organized to be back in the workforce is the way to go. You will need to wrap up the job search: i.e. put your tackle away, take a decent shower, thank your support group, and recover from the beating – all of that takes a bit. Job seeking is brutal and some space for recovery is essential once it is over. Also, throw in some time to celebrate, you have earned it! Maybe treat yourself to a nice fish dinner (LOL)!

Meanwhile, as you continue to look for work, be assured that you are not alone and that you will make it to the other side, one day you will be employed again. Do the things you need to do to survive this time – and hopefully you will be pleasantly surprised as you uncover the next step in your employment journey.

When you step out into your new journey, prepare all you have learned into some touch-stone or map for yourself in case you ever wind up back in the job searching reality. Leave yourself some tips of the "best things I did" and "things to avoid" so that you can pick up where you left off if your new position does not work out soon, or in ten years. The tools of the search will change, you will change, and the people who are searching will be different faces, but you have accomplished much – do not lose sight of that. Then, even while working - keep your resume up-to-date, maintain your self-care, foster your network, read (and work) the books on how to land the perfect job for you, bank some cushion money, keep a list of companies you would like to find out more about, and remember to avoid the "I wish I would haves" that your current job search uncovered for you. In our rapidly changing economy, you will be glad you put that map in place. You might even share what you learn with others – as I have done for you here.

I wish you the best as you search. Feel free to reach out to me if you have any questions about the materials in this book. Also, I frequently coach people on all aspects of the job search, so let me know if I can help.

I hope you catch a great job – and have a great story to tell about how you landed it. I know you will!

Pam Otten

ottenpam@gmail.com

https://www.linkedin.com/in/ottenpam/

www.ingramcontent.com/pod-product-compliance
Lightning Source LLC
Chambersburg PA
CBHW070806220526
45466CB00002B/566